Simple Tips for

Simple Living

for Couples

New Leaf Press

First Printing: March 2004

Cover by Left Coast Design, Portland, OR
Interior design by Brent Spurlock
Edited by Jim Fletcher and Roger Howerton

ISBN: 0-89221-572-0
Library of Congress Catalog Card Number: 2003116022

Please visit our web site for more great titles:
www.newleafpress.net

New Leaf Press

A special gift for you

To

_____

From

_____

Simple Living

Section 1

Off to a Good Start

1

True Love Takes Time

It takes only a minute to get a crush on someone, an hour to like someone, and a day to love someone, but it takes a lifetime to forget someone.

Love at first sight is easy to understand. It's when two people have been looking at each other for years that it becomes a miracle.

– Sam Levenson

Better is the end of a thing than the beginning thereof.
– Ecclesiastes 7:8

*And Jacob loved Rachel; and said, I will serve thee seven years
for Rachel thy younger daughter. And Laban said, It is better that
I give her to thee, than that I should give her to another man:
abide with me. And Jacob served seven years for Rachel; and
they seemed unto him but a few days, for the love he had to her.*
– Genesis 29:18-20

*Love never promises instant gratification,
only ultimate fulfillment.*

– Anonymous

2

Every Date Is a Potential Mate

In the *South Shore News*, Kathleen
Kroll Driscoll was writing about dating
and how a woman can figure out what
kind of person she's going out with.

She says:

A theater is an interesting
place to analyze someone new in
your life. Does he have a phobia
about sitting on the aisle? When
everyone else is sniffling and

crying, is he busy unwrapping licorice and covering up emotions? Does he hog the communal armrest? Does he put his feet on the seat in front? Is he reluctant to ask people to move over one seat so the two of you can sit together? Everything you want to know about your potential mate can be discerned during a movie.

Who we really are cannot be hidden. And the little things often reveal the most.[1]

Love is blind — marriage is the eye-opener.

– Pauline Thomason

In dating, the first hurdle is getting the person to whom you're attracted to ask you out. Or, if you're a guy, getting up the courage to ask someone out. Before I ever asked my wife out on a date, I wanted to find out more about her. More importantly, I wanted to find out more about her character.

I gathered firewood. I asked her roommates about her. I went places I knew she would be so I could observe her in certain situations. If you want to start a lasting fire, you need some kindling, lighter fluid and some serious firewood. I consider physical attraction and sexual passion as kindling and lighter fluid. However, if a fire is built only with kindling and lighter fluid, it will produce a roaring blaze but will go out in a matter of minutes. To build a lasting fire, you'll need firewood, which means putting issues related to spiritual depth and character into the proper context as you date.[2]

Let us choose to us judgment: let us know among
ourselves what is good.
– Job 34:4

3

Be Sure You Know What the Other Is Talking About

An English lady, while visiting Switzerland to check on a teaching position, was looking for a room, and she asked the schoolmaster if he could recommend any to her. He took her to see several rooms, and when everything was settled, the lady returned to her home to make the final preparations to move.

When she arrived home, the thought suddenly occurred to her that she had not seen a water closet [a euphemism for bathroom] around the place. So she immediately wrote a note to the schoolmaster asking him if there were a "W.C." around. The schoolmaster was a very poor student of English, so he asked the parish priest if he could help in the matter. Together they tired to discover the meaning of the letters W.C., and the only solution they could find for the letters was letters was a Wayside Chapel. The schoolmaster then wrote to the English lady the following note:

Dear Madam:

I take great pleasure in informing you that the

W.C. is situated nine miles from the house you occupy, in the center of a beautiful grove of pine trees surrounded by lovely grounds. It is capable of holding 229 people and it is open on Sunday and Thursday only. As there are a great number of people and they are expected during the summer months, I would suggest that you come early: although there is plenty of standing room as a rule. You will no doubt be glad to hear that a good number of people bring their lunch and make a day of it, while others who can afford to go by car arrive just in time. I would especially recommend that your ladyship go on Thursday when there is a musical accompaniment.

It may interest you to know that my daughter was married in the W.C. and it was there that she met her husband. I can remember the rush there was for seats. There were ten people to a seat ordinarily occupied by one. It was wonderful to see the expression on their faces. The newest attraction is a bell donated by a wealthy resident of the district. It rings every time a person enters. A bazaar is to be held to provide plush seats for all the people, since they feel it is a long felt need. My wife is rather delicate, so she can't attend regularly. I shall be delighted to reserve the best seat for you if you wish, where you will be seen by all. For the children, there is a special time and place so that they will not disturb the elders. Hoping to have been of service to you, I remain,

   The Schoolmaster.

I know you believe you understand what you think I said, but I'm not sure you realize that what you heard is not what I meant.

— Anonymous

Let what you say be simply yes or no.
– Matthew 5:37 (RSV)

Let your speech always be gracious, seasoned with salt.
– Colossians 4:6

Simple Living

Tip

4

Don't Rush into Commitments

Sex is a good thing. It must be, if God created it! The only way to keep it a "good thing" is to follow God's guidelines. God will reward you if you choose to honor Him, and save sex for its proper time and place — your marriage.[3]

And endurance produces character, and character produces hope, and hope does not disappoint us, because God's love has been poured into our hearts through the Holy Spirit which has been given to us.
– Romans 5:4-5 (RSV)

But if we hope for what we do not see,
we wait for it with patience.
– Romans 8:25

I'm proud to say that I am a virgin, and I don't hide the strength God has given me. You have to learn to respect yourself before you can start respecting other people.

– A.C. Green, basketball star on the Los Angeles Lakers' 2000 World Championship Team

Making love is a wonderful thing between a husband and wife in marriage. God promises that He will bless that relationship. The marriage relationship will not be as fulfilling if you don't abstain from sex before marriage. There is a danger of bringing emotional scars into marriage if you have sex in relationships prior to marriage.

– Brett Butler, former Los Angeles Dodger

5

Never Lose Hope

The school system in a large city
had a program to help children keep
up with their school work during
stays in the city's hospitals. One day
a teacher who was assigned to the
program received a routine call asking
her to visit a particular child. She took
the child's name and room number
and talked briefly with the child's
regular class teacher. "We're studying

nouns and adverbs in his class now," the regular teacher said, "and I'd be grateful if you could help him understand them so he doesn't fall too far behind."

The hospital program teacher went to see the boy that afternoon. No one had mentioned to her that the boy had been badly burned and was in great pain. Upset at the sight of the boy, she stammered as she told him, "I've been sent by your school to help you with nouns and adverbs." When she left she felt she hadn't accomplished much.

But the next day, a nurse asked her, "What did you do to that boy?" The teacher felt she must have done something wrong and began to apologize. "No, no," said the nurse. "You don't know what I mean. We've been worried about that little boy, but ever since yesterday, his whole attitude has changed. He's fighting back, responding to treatment. It's as though he's decided to live."

Two weeks later the boy explained that he had completely given up hope until the teacher arrived. Everything changed when he came to a simple realization. He expressed it this way: "They wouldn't send a teacher to work on nouns and adverbs with a dying boy, would they?" [4]

Now faith is the substance of things hoped for, the evidence of things not seen.

– Hebrews 11:1

Be of good courage, and he shall strengthen your heart, all ye that hope in the LORD.

– Psalm 31:24

Maybe when the door of happiness closes, another opens, but often times we look so long at the closed door that we don't see the one that has been opened for us.

– Anonymous

6

Look on the Inside as Well as the Outside

When you think of someone buying a luxury home with a price tag of more than $300,000, you expect the new home to be of high quality. Such is not always the case, writes Julie Iovine in the *Chicago Tribune*. The preliminary designs for the new home of Michael Eisner, the head of Disney, included one wall that was so thin it would have buckled under its own weight. The $40 million new home of one billionaire software developer had pine siding so vulnerable to decay it started to rot before the home was even completed. It is easy for buyers to mistake luxury for quality. Experts in the home building industry say that "most buyers agonize over the wrong things."

Tom Kligerman, a Manhattan architect, says many buyers "find it boring to spend money on foundations and stud walls. They'd rather spend it on what they can see."

A builder of luxury homes said, "It appears that what sells houses depends on having a tub large enough for at least two people, and probably more; flashy stairs . . . and other glitzy, totally unnecessary elements, as opposed to spatial or constructional quality."

As it is with homes, so it is with people. Too many people put all their effort into image and appearance and pay no attention to the quality of their character.[5]

You can tell a lot about a fellow's character by his way of eating jellybeans.

– Ronald Reagan

But the LORD said to Samuel, "Do not look on his appearance or on the height of his stature, . . . for the LORD sees not as man sees; man looks on the outward appearance, but the LORD looks on the heart."
– 1 Samuel 16:7 (RSV)

Judge not according to the appearance, but judge righteous judgment.
– John 7:24

7

Find Someone Who Makes
Your Heart Smile

John Blanchard's interest in her
had begun a year before in a Florida
library. Taking a book off the shelf
he found himself intrigued, not with
the words of the book, but with the
notes penciled in the margin. The soft
handwriting reflected a thoughtful
soul and insightful mind. In the
front of the book, he discovered the

previous owner's name, Miss Hollis Maynell. With time and effort, he located her address. She lived in New York City. He wrote her a letter introducing himself and inviting her to correspond. The next day he was shipped overseas for service in World War II, but during the next year, the two grew to know each other through the mail. Each letter was a seed falling on a fertile heart. A romance was budding. Blanchard requested a photograph, but she refused. She felt that if he really cared, it wouldn't matter what she looked like.

When the day finally came for him to return from Europe, they scheduled their first meeting — 7 p.m. at Grand Central Station in New York. "You'll recognize me," she wrote, "by the red rose I'll be wearing on my lapel." So here he was in the station looking for a girl whose heart he loved, but whose face he'd never seen.

A young woman came toward him, her figure long and slim. Her blonde hair lay back in curls from her delicate ears; her eyes were blue as flowers. Her lips and chin had a gentle firmness, and in her pale blue dress she was like springtime come alive. He started toward her, entirely forgetting to notice that she was not wearing a rose. And then he saw Hollis Maynell.

She was standing almost directly behind the girl. A woman well past 40, she had graying hair tucked under a worn hat. She was more than plump, her thick-ankled feet thrust into low-heeled shoes. Her pale, plump face was gentle and sensible, her gray eyes had a warm and kindly twinkle. He did not hesitate. His fingers gripped the small worn blue leather copy of the book that was to identify him to her.

This would not be love, but it would be something precious, something perhaps even better than love, a friendship for which he had been and must ever be grateful. He squared his shoulders and saluted and held out the book to the woman, even though while he spoke he felt choked by the bitterness of his disappointment.

"I'm Lieutenant John Blanchard, and you must be

Miss Maynell. I am so glad you could meet me. May I take you to dinner?"

The woman's face broadened into a tolerant smile. "I don't know what this is about, Son," she answered, "but the young lady in the blue dress who just went by begged me to wear this rose on my coat. And she said if you were to ask me out to dinner, I should tell you that she is waiting for you in the big restaurant across the street. She said it was some kind of test!"

*Let him not trust in vanity, deceiving
himself; for vanity will be his
recompense.*
– Job 15:31 (RHV)

*And they that know thy name will put
their trust in thee: for thou, LORD, hast
not forsaken them that seek thee.*
– Psalm 9:10

*Don't go for looks; they can deceive. Don't go for wealth; even
that fades away. Find the one who makes your heart smile.*

– Anonymous

8

Learn to Appreciate Your Mate

Maybe God wanted us to meet the wrong people before meeting the right one so that when we finally meet the right person, we will know how to be grateful for that gift.

Maybe it is true that we don't know what we have got until we lose it, but it is also true that we don't know what we've been missing until it arrives.

– Anonymous

Every good gift and every perfect gift is from above, and cometh down from the Father of lights, with whom is no variableness, neither shadow of turning.

– James 1:17

Flattery is from the teeth out. Sincere appreciation is from the heart out.

– Dale Carnegie

Happiness lies for those who cry, those who hurt, those who have searched, and those who have tried, for only they can appreciate the importance of people who have touched their lives.

– Anonymous

Simple Living

Tip

9

**Keep a Positive Attitude and
Laugh a Little**

The following questions about love
and marriage were asked of children,
with some hilarious results.

How do you decide whom to marry?

You got to find somebody who
likes the same stuff. Like, if you like
sports, she should like it that you like
sports, and she should keep the chips
and dip coming. — *Alan, age 10*

No person really decides before they grow up who they're going to marry. God decides it all way before, and you get to find out later who you're stuck with.

— *Kirsten, age 10*

What is the right age to get married?

Twenty-three is the best age because you know the person FOREVER by then. — *Camille, age 10*

No age is good to get married at. You got to be a fool to get married. — *Freddie, age 6*

How can a stranger tell if two people are married?

You might have to guess, based on whether they seem to be yelling at the same kids. — *Derrick, age 8*

What do you think your mom and dad have in common?

Both don't want any more kids. — *Lori, age 8*

What do most people do on a date?

Dates are for having fun, and people should use them to get to know each other. Even boys have something to say if you listen long enough. — *Lynnette, age 8*

On the first date, they just tell each other lies and

that usually gets them interested enough to go for a second date. — *Martin, age 10*

What would you do on a first date that was turning sour?

I'd run home and play dead. The next day I would call all the newspapers and make sure they wrote about me in all the dead columns. — *Craig, age 9*

When is it okay to kiss someone?

When they're rich. — *Pam, age 7*

The law says you have to be eighteen, so I wouldn't want to mess with that. — *Curt, age 7*

The rule goes like this: If you kiss someone, then you should marry them and have kids with them. It's the right thing to do. — *Howard, age 8*

Is it better to be single or married?

It's better for girls to be single but not for boys. Boys need someone to clean up after them. — *Anita, age 9*

How would the world be different if people didn't get married?

There sure would be a lot of kids to explain, wouldn't there? — *Kelvin, age 8*

How would you make a marriage work?

Tell your wife that she looks pretty, even if she looks like a truck. — *Ricky, age 10*

A merry heart maketh a cheerful countenance.
– Proverbs 15:13

Children seldom misquote you. In fact, they usually repeat word for word what you shouldn't have said.

– Anonymous

10

Learn to Listen

The story is told of Franklin
Roosevelt, who often endured long
receiving lines at the White House. He
complained that no one really paid
any attention to what was said.

One day, during a reception, he
decided to try an experiment. To each
person who passed down the line
and shook his hand, he murmured, "I

murdered my grandmother this morning."

The guests responded with phrases like, "Marvelous! Keep up the good work. We are proud of you. God bless you, sir."

It was not till the end of the line, while greeting the ambassador from Bolivia, that his words were actually heard. Nonplussed, the ambassador leaned over and whispered, "I'm sure she had it coming."

> *A man is already halfway in love with*
> *any woman who listens to him.*
> – Brendan Francis Behan

Expect Some Heartache

In December 1914 . . . [on a] particular evening, spontaneous combustion had broken out in the film room [of Thomas Edison's laboratory]. Within minutes all the packing compounds, celluloid for records and film, and other flammable goods were in flames.

Fire companies from eight surrounding towns arrived, but the heat was so intense and the water pressure so low that the attempt to douse the flames was futile. Everything was destroyed. . . . With all his assets going up in a whoosh (although the damage exceeded two million dollars, the buildings were only insured for $238,000 because they were made of concrete and thought to be fireproof), would his spirit be broken?

The inventor's 24-year-old son, Charles, searched frantically for his father. He finally found him, calmly watching the fire, his face glowing in the reflection, his white hair blowing in the wind. "My heart ached for him," said Charles. "He was 67 — no longer a young man — and everything was going up in flames.

"When he saw me, he shouted, 'Charles, where's your mother?' When I told him I didn't know, he said, 'Find her. Bring her here. She will never see anything like this as long as she lives.' " The next morning, Edison looked at the ruins and said, "There is great value in disaster. All our mistakes are burned up. Thank God we can start anew." Three weeks after the fire, Edison managed to deliver the first phonograph.[6]

Love begins with a smile, grows with a kiss and ends with a tear.

— Anonymous

Then said he unto the disciples, It is impossible but that offences will come.

– Luke 17:1

The course of true love never did run smooth.

– William Shakespeare

12

Be Submissive

Then there's the story of the young woman who wanted to go to college, but her heart sank when she read the question on the application blank that asked, "Are you a leader?"

Being both honest and conscientious, she wrote, "No," and returned the application, expecting the worst. To her surprise, she received this letter from the college:

Dear Applicant:

A study of the application forms reveals that this year our college will have 1,452 new leaders. We are accepting you because we feel it is imperative that they have at least one follower.

Dean of Admissions

Be subject to one another out of reverence for Christ.
– Ephesians 5:21 (RSV)

Simple Living
Section 2

Loves Me,
Loves Me Not

13

Forgiveness Begets Lasting Relationships

Sociology professor Dr. Elaine Walster has studied the differences between "passionate" and "compassionate" love, and interviewed or observed more than 100,000 persons. She found that, for most couples, intense passion lasts six months to two and a half years. Clearly, for love to persist, it has to move beyond that first romantic frenzy into a warm intensity of deep friendship. Forgiveness is the capacity to accept reality as different from what one expected. Forgiveness of a person is the acceptance of one who has qualities that one, if given the chance, would not naturally accept. Forgiveness carries one into a dimension of life that is beyond where we would be if left alone.[7]

> For if ye forgive men their trespasses, your heavenly
> Father will also forgive you: But if ye forgive not men their
> trespasses, neither will your Father forgive your trespasses.
> – Matthew 6:14-15

> Forgiveness is an act of the will, and the will can function
> regardless of the temperature of the heart.
>
> – Corrie Ten Boom

Tip

14

Let Go of the Past

Forget each kindness that you do
as soon as you have done it. Forget the
praise that falls to you the moment
you have won it. Forget the slander
that you hear before you can repeat
it. Forget each slight, each spite, each
sneer, whenever you may meet it.

Remember every promise made
and keep it to the letter. Remember
those who lend you aid and be a

grateful debtor. Remember all the happiness that comes your way in living.

Forget each worry and distress; be hopeful and forgiving. Remember good, remember truth, remember heaven is above you.

And you will find, through age and youth, that many will love you.

Forget about the consequences of failure. Failure is only a temporary change in direction to set you straight for your next success.

– Denis Waitley

15

Learn the Difference between Romance and Love

Romance is flattering attentions;

Love is genuine thoughtfulness.

Romance is suspense, anticipation,

 surprise;

Love is dependability.

Romance is tingling, excitement;

Love is tenderness, constancy,

 being cherished.

Romance is delicious;

Love nourishes.

Romance can't last;

Love can't help it.

Romance is seeking perfection;

Love is forgiving faults.

Romance is fleeting;

Love is long.

Romance is the anguish of waiting for the phone
to ring to bring you a voice that will utter
endearments;

Love is the anguish of waiting for a call that will
assure you someone else is happy and safe.

Romance is eager, striving always to appear attractive to each other;

Love is two people who find beauty in each other no matter how they look.

Romance is dancing in the moonlight, gazing deep into desired eyes across a candlelit table;

Love is saying "You're tired, honey, I'll get up this time," and stumbling through the darkness to warm a bottle or to comfort a frightened child.

In real love you want the other person's good. In romantic love, you want the other person.

– Margaret Anderson

Charity suffereth long, and is kind.
– 1 Corinthians 13:4

Infatuation is when you think he's as sexy as Robert Redford, as smart as Henry Kissinger, as noble as Ralph Nader, as funny as Woody Allen, and as athletic as Jimmy Conners. Love is when you realize that he's as sexy as Woody Allen, as smart as Jimmy Connors, as funny as Ralph Nader, as athletic as Henry Kissinger and nothing like Robert Redford – but you'll take him anyway.

– Judith Viorst

16

Learn the Meaning of Happiness

Guys, just remember, if you get lucky, if you make a lot of money, if you get out and buy a lot of stuff — it's gonna break. You got your biggest, fanciest mansion in the world. It has air conditioning. It's got a pool. Just think of all the pumps that are going to go out. Or go to a yacht basin any place in the world. Nobody is smiling, and I'll tell you why. Something broke that morning. The generator's out; the microwave oven doesn't work. . . . Things just don't mean happiness.[8]

Happy is that people, that is in such a case: yea, happy is that people, whose God is the LORD.
— Psalm 144:15

For a man's life consisteth not in the abundance of the things which he possesseth.
— Luke 12:15

The happiest of people don't necessarily have the best of everything; they just make the most of everything that comes along their way.
— Anonymous

The Differences in Men and Women Are More Than Physical

Jan: Did you get a new haircut?

Christy: Yes, I did. Thanks for noticing.

Jan: Oh! That's so cute!

Christy: Do you think so? I wasn't sure after my hairdresser gave me the mirror. I mean, you don't think it's too fluffy looking?

Jan: Oh no! No, it's perfect. I'd love to get my hair cut like that, but I think my face is too wide. I'm pretty much stuck with this stuff I think.

Christy: Are you serious? I think your face is adorable. And you could easily get one of those layer cuts. That would look so cute, I think. I was actually going to do that except that I was afraid it would accent my long neck.

Jan: Oh, that's funny! I would love to have your neck!

Christy: Are you kidding? I know girls that would love to have your shoulders. Everything drapes so well on you. I mean, look at my arms, see how short they are? If I had your shoulders I could get clothes to fit me so much easier.

Meanwhile....

Jeff: Haircut?

Matt: Yeah.

Women and cats will do as they please and men and dogs should relax and get used to the idea.

– Robert Anson Heinlein

Whose adorning let it not be that outward adorning of plaiting the hair, and of wearing of gold, or of putting on of apparel; But let it be the hidden man of the heart, in that which is not corruptible, even the ornament of a meek and quiet spirit, which is in the sight of God of great price.
For after this manner in the old time the holy women also, who trusted in God, adorned themselves.
– 1 Peter 3:3-5

Be strong and conduct yourselves like men.
– 1 Samuel 4:9 (NKJV)

18

Don't Make Mountains Out of Molehills

On Thursday, January 24, 2002, Derek Guille broadcast this story on his afternoon program on ABC radio.

In March of 1999, a man living in Kandos, Australia, received a bill for his as-yet-unused gas line stating that he owed $0.00. He ignored it and threw it away. In April he received another bill and threw that one away too.

The following month the gas company

sent him a very nasty note stating they were going to cancel his gas line if he didn't send them $0.00 by return mail. He called them, talked to them, and they said it was a computer error and they would take care of it.

The following month he decided that it was about time that he tried out the troublesome gas line figuring that if there was usage on the account it would put an end to this ridiculous predicament. However, when he went to use the gas, it had been cut off. He called the gas company who apologized for the computer error once again and said that they would take care of it. The next day, he got a bill for $0.00 stating that payment was now overdue.

Assuming that, having spoken to them the previous day, the latest bill was yet another mistake, he ignored it, trusting that the company would be as good as their word and sort the problem out.

The next month he got a bill for $0.00. This bill also stated that he had 10 days to pay his account or the company would have to take steps to recover the debt.

Finally giving in, he thought he would beat the company at their own game and mailed them a check for $0.00. The computer duly processed his account and returned a statement to the effect that he now owed the gas company nothing at all.

A week later, the manager of the Mudgee branch of

the Westpac Banking Corporation called him and asked what he was doing writing checks for $0.00. After a lengthy explanation, the bank manager replied that the $0.00 check had caused their check processing software to fail. The bank could therefore not process ANY checks they had received from ANY of their customers that day because the check for $0.00 had caused the computer to crash.

The following month, the man received a letter from the gas company claiming that his check had bounced and that he now owed them $0.00 and unless he sent a check by return mail they would take immediate steps to recover the debt. At this point, the man decided to file a debt harassment claim against the gas company.

It took him nearly two hours to convince the clerks at the local courthouse that he was not joking. They subsequently assisted him in the drafting of statements which were considered substantive evidence of the aggravation and difficulties he had been forced to endure during this debacle. The matter was heard in the Magistrate's Court in Mudgee and the outcome was that the gas company was ordered to:

1] Immediately rectify their computerized accounts system or show cause, within 10 days, why the matter should not be referred to a higher court for consideration under company law.

2] Pay the bank dishonor fees incurred by the man.

3] Pay the bank dishonor fees incurred by all the Westpac clients whose checks had bounced on the day the computer crashed.

4] Pay the claimant's court costs; and

5] Pay the claimant a total of $1,500 per month for the five-month period March to July inclusive as compensation for the aggravation they had caused their client to suffer.

All this was over $0.00 — nothing.

I would have you wise as to what is good, and
guileless as to what is evil.
– Romans 16:19 (NKJV)

19

Try To See Things from the Other's Point of View

Leith Anderson, a pastor, shared an experience that throws light upon this truth. As a boy, he grew up outside of New York City and was an avid fan of the Brooklyn Dodgers. One day his father took him to a World Series game between the Dodgers and the Yankees. He was so excited, and he just knew the Dodgers would trounce the Yankees. Unfortunately, the Dodgers never got on base, and his excitement was shattered.

Years later he was engrossed in a conversation with a man who was a walking sports almanac. Leith told him about the first major league game he attended and added, "It was such a disappointment. I was a Dodger fan and the Dodgers never got on base."

The man said, "You were there? You were at the game when Don Larsen pitched the first perfect game in all of World Series history?"

Leith replied, "Yeah, but uh, we lost." He then realized that he had been so caught up in his team's defeat that he missed out on the fact that he was a witness to a far greater page of history.[9]

Before you criticize someone, walk a mile in his shoes. That way, if he gets angry, he'll be a mile away — and barefoot.

– Sarah Jackson

Let nothing be done through strife or vainglory; but in lowliness of mind let each esteem other better than themselves.
– Philippians 2:3

Be kindly affectioned one to another with brotherly love; in honour preferring one another.
– Romans 12:10

There Is a Reason for Everything — Good and Bad

Amy Carmichael, who would become one of the world's greatest missionaries, was born in December of 1867 in Northern Ireland. Her parents loved the Lord, and Amy was blessed to have been brought up in a godly home. Her parents had taught her about prayer, and how to pray. They told her, "Ask God, Amy, if you want anything badly. Share it with Him and He'll always give you an answer."

The young Irish girl had brown eyes, and wanted more than anything to have blue eyes like her mother. Remembering what her parents had taught her about prayer, one night she prayed that God would give her beautiful blue eyes. She prayed earnestly, and the next morning, she jumped out of bed excitedly and ran to the mirror. Looking closely, she saw no change in the color of her eyes and sorrowfully told her mother that God had not answered her prayer. Her mother consoled her by telling her that God had indeed answered her prayer — sometimes He answers with a no. She continued to tell Amy that He had good reason to have given her brown eyes instead of blue, even if that reason was not apparent.

Amy grew up and became a missionary to India. She had not been in that country long when she discovered the atrocious practice of forcing young girls to prostitute themselves in the Hindu temples to earn money for the false gods. Amy felt such compassion for these girls that she became a kidnapper. She would stain her face and other exposed areas of her skin with coffee and put on an Indian sari to enter into the temple area where foreign women would have been prohibited. Blue eyes would have definitely betrayed her nationality, but brown eyes allowed her to move in and out, unnoticed.

God protected her, and her rescue operation continued for 13 years. Once, upon rescuing a five-year-old girl, the girl's parents wanted their daughter back. The girl would surely have been abused, so Amy arranged for the girl's "disappearance." The parents brought charges of kidnapping against her, and she faced a seven-year prison term. However, before the sentence could be imposed, a telegram arrived with the words, "Criminal case dismissed," although there was no explanation of the origination of this telegram. Suffice it to say that God's hand was on the life of this brown-eyed woman, who had so wanted blue eyes.

May you have enough happiness to make you sweet, enough trials to make you strong, enough sorrow to keep you human, enough hope to make you happy.
– Anonymous

And we know that all things work together for good to them that love God, to them who are the called according to his purpose.
– Romans 8:28

For my thoughts are not your thoughts, neither are your ways my ways, saith the LORD.
– Isaiah 55:8

Never Bear a Grudge

A story tells that two friends were walking through the desert. During some point of the journey they had an argument, and one friend slapped the other one in the face. The one who got slapped was hurt, but without saying anything, wrote in the sand: "Today my best friend slapped me in the face."

They kept on walking until they found an oasis, where they decided to take a bath. The one who had been slapped got stuck in the mire and started drowning, but the friend saved him. After he recovered from the near drowning, he wrote on a stone: "Today my best friend saved my life."

The friend who had slapped and saved his best friend asked him, "After I hurt you, you wrote in the sand and now, you write on a stone; why?"

The other friend replied, "When someone hurts us we should write it down in sand where winds of forgiveness can erase it away. But, when someone does something good for us, we must engrave it in stone where no wind can ever erase it."

Let not the sun go down upon your wrath.
– Ephesians 4:26

Simple Living

Tip

22

Learn What Love Really Is

What is love?

It is silence — when your words
would hurt.

It is patience — when the other
person is curt.

It is deafness — when a scandal flows.

It is thoughtfulness — for other's woes.

It is promptness — when stern
duty calls.

It is courage — when misfortune falls.

Is it love? Probably not, if it . . .

- Assumes the other person will change to please you.

- Causes feelings of insecurity or jealousy.

- Appeared as "love at first sight."

- Is easily forgotten when the other person is not
  around.

- Makes you feel "stressed out" when you're together.

- Consumes your life.

- Is selfish.

- Seems to have peaked and is diminishing.

- Limits other friendships.

- Is based on your partner's appearance.

- Is based on feelings of possessiveness.

- Has sexual gratification as its main goal.

- Pressures you to do things you don't want to do.

- Blinds you to your partner's faults.

Is it love? Maybe, if it . . .

- Accepts the other person as he or she is.

- Builds trust.

- Started as friendship and grows over time.

- Lasts even when distance separates you.

- Makes you feel relaxed and at ease with each other.

- Allows you to do things without your partner.

- Makes you place your partner's needs before
  your own.

- Gets stronger as time goes on.

- Allows you to have friends of both genders.

- Considers appearance as only part of the attraction.

- Recognizes the other person's individuality.

- Is rewarding without a sexual component.

- Allows you to reject things that make you uncomfortable.

- Accepts your partner's faults.

How canst thou say, I love thee, when thine heart is not with me?
– Judges 16:15

You don't love a woman because she is beautiful,
she is beautiful because you love her.

– Anonymous

Learn and Understand the Imbalance of Conversation between Men and Women

In a Harvard study of several hundred preschoolers, researchers discovered an interesting phenomenon. As they taped the children's playground conversation, they realized that all the sounds coming from little girls' mouths were recognizable words.

However, only 60 percent of the sounds coming from little boys were recognizable. The other 40 percent were yells and sound effects like "Vrrrooooom!" "Aaaaagh!" "Toot toot!"

This difference persists into adulthood. Communication experts say that the average woman speaks over 25,000 words a day while the average man speaks only a little over 10,000. What does this mean in marital terms? On average a wife will say she needs to spend 45 minutes to an hour each day in meaningful conversation with her husband. What does her husband sitting next to her say is enough time for meaningful conversation? Fifteen to twenty minutes — once or twice a week! [10]

Give ye ear, and hear my voice; hearken, and hear my speech.
— Isaiah 28:23

Simple Living
Tip

24

Be Sincere

Dearest Jimmy,

No words could ever express the great unhappiness I've felt since breaking our engagement. Please say you'll take me back. No one could ever take your place in my heart, so please forgive me. I love you, I love you, I love you!

Yours forever,

Marie

P.S. And congratulations on winning the state lottery.

That ye may approve things that are excellent; that ye may be sincere and without offence till the day of Christ.
–Philippians 1:10

Then shall he answer them, saying, Verily I say unto you, Inasmuch as ye did it not to one of the least of these, ye did it not to me.
– Matthew 25:45

The most exhausting thing in life is being insincere.
– Anne Morrow Lindbergh

Know What the Bible Says about Love

Though I speak with the tongues of men and of angels, and have not love, I am become as sounding brass, or a tinkling cymbal. And though I have the gift of prophecy, and understand all mysteries, and all knowledge; and though I have all faith, so that I could remove mountains, and have not love, I am nothing. And though I bestow all my goods to feed the poor, and though I give my body to be burned, and have not love, it profiteth me nothing.

Love suffereth long, and is kind; love envieth not; love vaunteth not itself, is not puffed up, Doth not behave itself unseemly, seeketh not her own, is not easily provoked, thinketh no evil; Rejoiceth not in iniquity, but rejoiceth in the truth; Beareth all things, believeth all things, hopeth all things, endureth all things.

Love never faileth: but whether there be prophecies, they shall fail; whether there be tongues, they shall cease; whether there be knowledge, it shall vanish away. For we know in part, and we prophesy in part.

But when that which is perfect is come, then that which is in part shall be done away. When I was a child, I spake as a child, I understood as a child, I thought as a child: but when I became a man, I put away childish things. For now we see through a glass, darkly; but then face to face: now I know in part; but then shall I know even as also I am known. And now abideth faith, hope, love, these three; but the greatest of these is love.

– 1 Corinthians 13 (KJV with love substituted for charity)

Now the end of the commandment is charity out of a pure heart, and of a good conscience, and of faith unfeigned.
– 1 Timothy 1:5

With all lowliness and gentleness, with longsuffering, bearing with one another in love.
– Ephesians 4:2 (NKJV)

Simple Living
Tip

26

Get to Know Your Mate

Six ways to learn everything you ever need to know about a man before you decide to marry him:

1) Watch him drive in heavy traffic.

2) Play tennis with him.

3) Listen to him talk to his mother when he doesn't know you're listening.

4) See how he treats those who serve him
   (waiters, maids).

5) Notice what he's willing to spend his money to buy.

6) Look at his friends.

And if you still can't make up your mind, then look at his shoes. A man who keeps his shoes in good repair generally tends to the rest of his life too.[11]

*For I know him, that he will command
his children and his household after
him, and they shall keep the way of the
LORD, to do justice and judgment.*
– Genesis 18:19

Memorize the Most Important Relationship Words

The SIX most important words:

"I admit I made a mistake."

The FIVE most important words:

"You did a good job."

The FOUR most important words:

"What do you think?"

The THREE most important words:

"I love you."

The TWO most important words:

"Thank you."

The ONE most important word:

"We."

The LEAST important word:

"I."

> *When negotiating, always listen to the other person's point of view and interests first. He or she may be willing to give you more than you expected.*
>
> – Brian Koslow

28

Never Try to Second Guess What the Other is Thinking

Let's say a guy named Roger is attracted to a woman named Elaine. He asks her out to dinner; she accepts; they have a pretty good time. A few nights later he asks her out again; and again they enjoy themselves. They continue to see each other regularly, and after a while neither one of them is seeing anybody else.

And then, one evening when they're driving home, a thought occurs to Elaine, and, without really thinking, she says it aloud: "Do you realize that, as of tonight, we've been seeing each other for exactly six months?"

And then there is silence in the car.

To Elaine, it seems like a very loud silence. She thinks to herself: *I wonder if it bothers him that I said that. Maybe he's been feeling confined by our relationship; maybe he thinks I'm trying to push him into some kind of obligation that he doesn't want, or isn't sure of.*

And Roger is thinking: *Wow! Six months.*

And Elaine is thinking: *But, hey, I'm not so sure*

I want this kind of relationship, either. Sometimes I wish I had a little more space, so I'd have time to think about whether I really want us to keep going the way we are, moving steadily toward. . . . I mean, where are we going? Are we just going to keep seeing each other at this level of intimacy? Are we heading toward marriage? Toward children? Toward a lifetime together? Am I ready for that level of commitment? Do I really even know this person?

And Roger is thinking: *So, that means it was . . . let's see . . . February when we started going out, which was right after I had the car at the dealer's, which means . . . let me check the odometer. . . . Whoa! I am way overdue for an oil change here.*

And Elaine is thinking: *He's upset. I can see it on his face. Maybe I'm reading this completely wrong. Maybe he wants more from our relationship, more intimacy, more commitment; maybe he has sensed, even before I sensed it, that I was feeling some reservations. Yes, I bet that's it. That's why he's so reluctant to say anything about his own feelings. He's afraid of being rejected.*

And Roger is thinking: *And I'm going to have them look at the transmission again. I don't care what those morons say, it's still not shifting right. And they better not try to blame it on the cold weather this time. What cold weather? It's 87 degrees and this thing is shifting* like a garbage truck, and I paid those incompetent thieves $600.

And Elaine is thinking: *He's angry. And I don't blame him. I'd be angry, too. I feel so guilty, putting him through this, but I can't help the way I feel. I'm just not sure.*

And Roger is thinking: *They'll probably say it's only a 90-day warranty . . . idiots.*

And Elaine is thinking: *Maybe I'm just too idealistic, waiting for a knight to come riding up on his white horse, when I'm sitting right next to a perfectly good person, a person I enjoy being with, a person I truly do care about, a person who seems to truly care about me*

— a person who is in pain because of my self-centered, schoolgirl romantic fantasy.

And Roger is thinking: *Warranty? They'd better not say its only a 90-day warranty.*

"Roger," Elaine says aloud.

"What?" says Roger, startled.

"Please don't torture yourself like this," she says, her eyes beginning to brim with tears. "Maybe I should never have . . . Oh my, I feel so. . . . (She breaks down, sobbing.)

"What?" says Roger.

"I'm such a fool," Elaine sobs. "I mean, I know there's no knight. I really know that. It's silly. There's no knight, and there's no horse."

"There's no horse?" says Roger.

"You think I'm a fool, don't you?" Elaine says.

"No!" says Roger, glad to finally know the correct answer.

"It's just that . . . it's that I . . . I need some time," Elaine says.

There is a 15-second pause while Roger, thinking as fast as he can, tries to come up with a safe response. Finally he comes up with one that he thinks might work. "Yes," he says.

Elaine, deeply moved, touches his hand. "Oh, Roger, do you really feel that way?" she says.

"What way?" says Roger.

"That way about time," says Elaine.

"Oh," says Roger. "Yes."

Elaine turns to face him and gazes deeply into his eyes, causing him to become very nervous about what she might say next, especially if it involves a horse. At last she speaks.

"Thank you, Roger," she says.

"Thank you," says Roger.

Then he takes her home, and she lies on her bed, a conflicted, tortured soul, and weeps until dawn.

When Roger gets back to his place, he opens a bag of Doritos, turns on the TV, and immediately becomes deeply involved in a rerun of a tennis match between two Czechoslovakians he never heard of. A tiny voice in the far recesses of his mind tells him that something major was going on back there in the car, but he is pretty sure there is no way he would ever understand what, and so he figures it's better if he doesn't think about it.

The next day Elaine will call her closest friend, or perhaps two of them, and they will talk about this situation for six straight hours. In painstaking detail, they will analyze everything she said and everything he said, going over it time and time again, exploring every word, expression, and gesture for nuances of meaning, considering every possible ramification. They will continue to discuss this subject, off and on, for weeks, maybe months, never reaching any definite conclusions, but never getting bored with it, either.

Meanwhile, Roger, while playing racquetball one day with a mutual friend of his and Elaine's, will pause just before serving, frown, and say, "Norm, did Elaine ever own a horse?"

And that's the difference between men and women.[12]

Two are better than one; because they
have a good reward for their labour.
– Ecclesiastes 4:9

29

Plan for the Future, Trusting God

The prospective father-in-law asked, "Young man, can you support a family?"

The surprised groom-to-be replied, "Well, no. I was just planning to support your daughter. The rest of you will have to fend for yourselves."

Never be afraid to trust an unknown future to a known God.

– Corrie Ten Boom

Ye ought to say, If the Lord will, we shall live, and do this, or that.
– James 4:15

And this will we do, if God permit.
– Hebrews 6:3

The Proposal Should Be Extraordinary

It was not your ordinary proposal. During the New York City Marathon, Terry O'Brien of New York had something special on his mind besides completing the 26.2-mile road race.

At mile 16, the 36 year old pulled out a ring and dropped to one knee in front of Janelle Billingsley, 30, standing at the curb. The pair had just celebrated their fourth year of dating.

"I was caught completely off guard," Billingsley said.

O'Brien's sweaty, disheveled appearance didn't sway her answer. "I said yes," Billingsley recalled. "I most definitely said yes."

Before she knew it, her betrothed was off and running again. He still had 10 miles to go.

"Up until the 16-mile mark, I was kind of giddy," O'Brien said. "Then I realized I still had a long way to go. The last leg was kind of tough."

Despite the short breather, O'Brien finished the race in 3 hours and 55 minutes.

How did he come up with the proposal idea? He said he was inspired on a training run.

"You have an awful lot of time to think about stuff when you're running 20 miles." No word if the wedding party will be wearing track shoes or not.[13]

The pleasantest part of a man's life is generally that which passes in courtship, provided his passion be sincere, and the party beloved, kind, with discretion. Love, desire, hope, all the pleasing motions of the soul, rise in the pursuit.

– Joseph Addison

*For this cause shall a man leave his father and mother, and
shall be joined unto his wife, and they two shall be one flesh.*
– Ephesians 5:31

*Whoso findeth a wife findeth a good thing, and
obtaineth favour of the LORD.*
– Proverbs 18:22

31

Never Gloat

On the day that news arrived in Washington that the war was over, a crowd gathered at the White House and a military band was playing some festive music. President Lincoln stood on the balcony of the White House and spoke. Instead of lashing out against the South, he spoke of the horrors of war being over. He spoke of families getting back together. He spoke of a time of peace. Then he said, "In a few moments I want the band to play and I'm going to tell them what I want them to play."

Of course, the band started getting the "Battle Hymn of The Republic" ready to play. This had been the theme song of the North throughout the Civil War. But Lincoln crossed them up. He stood there and said: "The band will now play the theme song of the people we have called our enemy. They are not our enemies any more! We are one people again. I want the band to play 'Dixie.' "

Historians say there was a long, awkward pause. The band didn't have the music to "Dixie," but they finally got together and played it. Instead of gloating and bragging, Lincoln showed compassion and forgiveness to the defeated South. A pompous attitude only adds insult to injury. It's unfortunate that Lincoln didn't live to head up the reconstruction. Our nation's history may have been significantly different with Lincoln at the helm during those crucial years.

You shouldn't gloat about anything you've done; you ought to keep going and find something better to do.

— David Packard

*Rejoice not when thine enemy falleth, and let not thine heart
be glad when he stumbleth.*
– Proverbs 24:17

*A prudent man concealeth knowledge: but the heart of fools
proclaimeth foolishness.*
– Proverbs 12:23

Learn the Golden Rule

Many years ago two boys were working their way through Stanford University. Their funds got desperately low, and the idea came to them to engage Padarewski for a piano recital. They would use the funds to help pay their board and tuition. The great pianist's manager asked for a guarantee of $2,000. The guarantee was a lot of money in those days, but the boys agreed and proceeded to promote the concert. They worked hard, only to find that they had grossed only $1,600. After the concert the two boys told the great artist the bad news. They gave him the entire $1,600, along with a promissory note for $400, explaining that they would earn the amount at the earliest possible moment and send the money to him. It looked like the end of their college careers.

"No, boys," replied Padarewski, "that won't do." Then, tearing the note in two, he returned the money to them as well. "Now," he told them, "take out of this $1,600 all of your expenses, and keep for each of you 10 percent of the balance for your work. Let me have the rest."

The years rolled by — World War I came and went. Padarewski, now premier of Poland, was striving to feed thousands of starving people in his native land. There was only one man in the world who could help him, Herbert Hoover, who was in charge of the U.S. Food and Relief Bureau. Hoover responded and soon thousands of tons of food were sent to Poland.

After the starving people were fed, Padarewski journeyed to Paris to thank Hoover for the relief sent him. "That's all right, Mr. Padarewski," was Hoover's reply. "Besides, you don't remember it, but you helped me once when I was a student at college, and I was in trouble." [14]

Therefore all things whatsoever ye would that men should do to you, do ye even so to them: for this is the law and the prophets.
– Matthew 7:12

Give, and it shall be given unto you; good measure, pressed down, and shaken together, and running over, shall men give into your bosom. For with the same measure that ye mete withal it shall be measured to you again.
– Luke 6:38

Always put yourself in the other's shoes. If you feel that it hurts you, it probably hurts the other person, too.
– Anonymous

33

Be Discreet

My sister, Becky, prepared a pasta dish for a dinner party she was giving. In her haste, however, she forgot to refrigerate the spaghetti sauce, and it sat on the counter all day. She was worried about spoilage, but it was too late to cook up another batch. She called the local Poison Control Center and voiced her concern. They advised Becky to boil the sauce again.

That night, the phone rang during dinner, and a guest volunteered to answer it. Her face dropped as she called out, "It's the Poison Control Center. They want to know how the spaghetti sauce turned out."[15]

A whisperer separateth chief friends.
– Proverbs 16:28

I have never been hurt by anything I didn't say.

– Calvin Coolidge

Discretion is the perfection of reason, and a guide to us in all the duties of life.

– Jean de La Bruyere

Simple Living

Section 3

The Best Years
of Our Lives

34

Treasure Your Wife

God made a wife to be a special blend

Of sweetheart, companion, helpmate
and friend.

She's a comfort and joy in time of strife,

One who gives meaning and purpose
to life.

She is the reason you dream and plan.

She gives you the faith to believe you can.

No one can measure a wife's true worth.

She's a taste of heaven right here on earth.

Husbands, love your wives, even as Christ also
loved the church, and gave himself for it.
– Ephesians 5:25

Let thy foundation be blessed: and rejoice
with the wife of thy youth.
– Proverbs 5:18

It's not true that married men live longer than
single men . . . it just seems that way.
– Anonymous

35

Admit When You're Wrong

To keep your marriage brimming,

With love in the loving cup

Whenever you're wrong, admit it

Whenever you're right, shut up![16]

One of the hardest things in this world is to admit you are wrong. And nothing is more helpful in resolving a situation than its frank admission.

– Benjamin Disraeli

He who guards his mouth and his tongue keeps himself from calamity.
– Proverbs 21:23

Confess your faults one to another, and pray one for another.
– James 5:16

Take Advice from an Experienced Couple

These rules are from a couple who reached their 50th anniversary and successfully made their marriage a promise for life. See how many of these are rules you live by:

1. Never be angry at the same time.

2. Never yell at each other unless the house is on fire.

3. If one of you has to win an argument, let it be your mate.

4. If you must criticize, do it lovingly.

5. Never bring up mistakes of the past.

6. Neglect the whole world rather than each other.

7. Never go to sleep with an argument unsettled.

8. At least once every day say a kind or complimentary word to your spouse.

9. When you have done something wrong, admit it and ask for forgiveness.

10. Remember it takes two to make a quarrel.

Conversation means being able to disagree and still continue the discussion.

– Dwight MacDonald

Know the Truth about Divorce Statistics

I heard it again on TV and radio this week … and from leaders that ought to know better. The old myth "one out of every two marriages ends in divorce." That is not true, never has been and never will be. Yet everyone who keeps perpetuating this falsehood is unwittingly encouraging divorce and destroying hope. Enough of this gloom, doom, and negativism.

Questions. Why should a couple work at building a great marriage when they've heard repeatedly that it doesn't work for at least half of the population? Why do we insist on painting the situation worse than it is?

Whence the problem? The Census Bureau noted that during one year 2.4 million marriages were reported. During the same 12-month period, there were 1.2 million divorces. So, presto, one out of every two marriages ends in divorce. Hardly. They forgot to include the great pool of existing marriages, 54 million of them. That produces quite a different conclusion.

Pollster Louis Harris concluded, "the idea that half of American marriages are doomed is one of the most specious pieces of statistical nonsense ever perpetuated in modern times. Only one out of eight marriages will end in divorce and in any single year only about two percent of existing marriages will break up."

Thus under attack, marriage is alive and well. God's great idea![17]

Divorce is an easy escape, many think. But . . . the guilt and loneliness they experience can be even more tragic than living with their problem.

– Billy Graham

Therefore shall a man leave his father and his mother, and shall cleave unto his wife: and they shall be one flesh.
– Genesis 2:24

Keep in Touch When You're Apart

A few years ago, the Harry S. Truman Library in Independence, Missouri, made public 1,300 recently discovered letters that the late President wrote to his wife, Bess, over the course of a half-century. Mr. Truman had a lifelong rule of writing to his wife every day they were apart. He followed this rule whenever he was away on official business or whenever Bess left

Washington to visit her beloved Independence.

Scholars are examining the letters for any new light they may throw on political and diplomatic history. For our part, we were most impressed by the simple fact that every day he was away, the President of the United States took time out from his dealing with the world's most powerful leaders to sit down and write a letter to his wife.[18]

That the communication of thy faith may become effectual by the acknowledging of every good thing which is in you in Christ Jesus.
– Philemon 1:6

Letter writing on the part of a busy man or woman is the quintessence of generosity.

– Agnes Repplier

Be Tactful

Perhaps you heard about the
husband who lacked tact. Early one
morning his wife left for a trip abroad...
and that very day their poodle died.
When she called home that evening, she
asked how everything was — and he
bluntly blurted out, "Well, the dog died!"
Shocked, she chided him through tears
for being so tactless, so strong.

"What should I have said?" he asked.

"You should've broken the news gently, perhaps in stages. When I called you from here in New York, you could have said, 'The dog is on the roof.' And the next day when I called you from London, 'He fell off the roof.' The following day from Paris, you could have told me, 'He is at the vet's...in the hospital.' And finally, from Rome, I could have then been informed, 'He died.' "

The husband paused and thought about the advice. His wife then asked, "By the way, how is Mother?"

He responded, "She's on the roof!"[19]

Tact: Putting it nicely, but not quite precisely.

– Norma Becket

40

Learn to Give

Californians Randy Curlee and Victoria Ingram became engaged in February 1994. According to the *Chicago Tribune*, a short time later, Randy received bad news from his doctor. Randy had suffered from diabetes since he was 12; he was now 46, and the doctor said the diabetes had ruined his kidneys. He would need a transplant to save his life.

Randy brought his fiancée, Victoria, to hear what the doctor was saying so she would understand how his diabetes would affect their future. The doctor said that each year only 4,000 kidneys become available to the 36,000 people who need a transplant. Usually family members provide the best match for a transplant, but none of Randy's family matched his profile well.

Victoria spoke up, "Why don't you test me?" The doctor gave her the tests, and the couple went home and forgot about it.

Then the phone rang. Randy's doctor reported that their immune systems were an identical match.

So the couple made plans to be married on October 11, 1994, and the next day to have the transplant surgery. At the last minute, the surgery had to be delayed because Victoria's kidney was nicked by a catheter during testing. But one month after becoming man and wife, in a five-and-a-half-hour operation at Sharp Memorial Hospital in San Diego, Victoria gave her husband, Randy, her left kidney. It was believed to be the first organ swap between husband and wife in the United States.

Randy and Victoria's marriage literally depended on her sacrifice for its survival. In a sense, so does every marriage. Marriages survive and thrive when spouses focus on what they can give to their partner more than on what they can get.[20]

Greater love hath no man than this, that a man lay down his life for his friends.
— John 15:13

And there came a certain poor widow, and she threw in two mites, which make a farthing.
And he called unto him his disciples, and saith unto them, Verily I say unto you, That this poor widow hath cast more in, than all they which have cast into the treasury: For all they did cast in of their abundance; but she of her want did cast in all that she had, even all her living.
— Mark 12:42-44

It is possible to give without loving, but it is impossible to love without giving.
— Richard Braunstein

Be Patient

An old missionary couple had
been working in Africa for years
and were returning to New York
to retire. They had no pension;
their health was broken; they were
defeated, discouraged, and afraid.
They discovered they were booked
on the same ship as President
Teddy Roosevelt, who was returning
from one of his big-game hunting

expeditions. No one paid any attention to them. They watched the fanfare that accompanied the president's entourage, with passengers trying to catch a glimpse of the great man.

As the ship moved across the ocean, the old missionary said to his wife, "Something is wrong. Why should we have given our lives in faithful service for God in Africa all these many years and have no one care a thing about us? Here this man comes back from a hunting trip and everybody makes much over him, but nobody gives two hoots about us."

"Dear, you shouldn't feel that way." his wife said.

He replied "I can't help it; it doesn't seem right."

When the ship docked in New York, a band was waiting to greet the president. The mayor and other dignitaries were there. The papers were full of the president's arrival. No one noticed this missionary couple. They slipped off the ship and found a cheap flat on the East Side, hoping the next day to see what they could do to make a living in the city.

That night the man's spirit broke. He said to his wife, "I can't take this; God is not treating us fairly." His wife replied, "Why don't you go in the bedroom and tell that to the Lord?"

A short time later, he came out from the bedroom, but now his face was completely different. His wife asked, "Dear, what happened?"

He said, "The Lord settled it with me. I told Him how bitter I was that the president should receive this tremendous homecoming, when no one met us as we returned home. And when I finished, it seemed as though the Lord put His hand on my shoulder and simply said; "But you're not home yet."

Wait on the LORD: be of good courage, and he shall strengthen thine heart: wait, I say, on the LORD.
– Psalm 27:14

They shall not be ashamed that wait for me.
– Isaiah 49:23

42

Stay Focused

When asked on his 50th wedding anniversary for his advice on marital bliss and longevity, Henry Ford replied, "Just the same as in the automobile business, stick to one model."

Infidelity and marital conflict are cancers that gnaw on the soul of mankind, twisting and warping innocent family members who can only stand and watch.

– James C. Dobson

*But you remain the same, and your years will never end.
The children of your servants will live in your presence; their
descendants will be established before you.*
– Psalm 102:27-28

*If any be blameless, the husband of one wife, having faithful
children not accused of riot or unruly.*
– Titus 1:6

43

Be Flexible

Openness is essentially the willingness to grow, a distaste for ruts, eagerly standing on tip-toe for a better view of what tomorrow brings.

A man once bought a new radio, brought it home, placed it on the refrigerator, plugged it in, turned it to WSM in Nashville (home of the Grand Ole Opry), and then pulled all the knobs off! He had already tuned in all he ever wanted or expected to hear.

Some marriages are "rutted" and rather dreary because either or both partners have yielded to the tyranny of the inevitable, "what has been will still be." Stay open to newness. Stay open to change.[21]

Old things are passed away; behold, all things are become new.
— 2 Corinthians 5:17

Success in marriage is more than finding the right person: it is being the right person.

— Robert Browning

44

Learn To Say "I Love You"

The teacher in our adult-education
creative-writing class told us to
write "I love you" in 25 words or less,
without using the words "I love you."
She gave us 15 minutes.

A woman in the class spent about
ten minutes looking at the ceiling and
wriggling in her seat. The last five
minutes she wrote frantically, and later
read us the results:

"Why, I've seen lots worse hairdos than that, honey."

"These cookies are hardly burned at all."

"Cuddle up — I'll get your feet warm."[22]

Let him kiss me with the kisses of his mouth:
for thy love is better than wine.
– Song of Solomon 1:2

Love doesn't make the world go 'round; love
is what makes the ride worthwhile.

– Franklin P. Jones

Simple Living
References

[1] Craig Brian Larson, *750 Engaging Illustrations for Preachers, Teachers, and Writers* (Grand Rapids, MI: Baker Books, 2002), p. 63, quoting from Kathleen Kroll Driscoll, Rockland (Massachusetts) *South Shore News*, as seen in *Reader's Digest* (November 1993), 145.

[2] *The Song of Solomon Conference*, Hudson Productions.

[3] George Martin and Scott Myers.

[4] *Bits & Pieces*, July 1991.

[5] Craig Brian Larson, *750 Engaging Illustrations for Preachers, Teachers, and Writers* (Grand Rapids, MI: Baker Books, 2002), p. 66, quoting from Julie V. Iovine, "Style over Substance," *Chicago Tribune*, March 29, 2997, sec. 4, p. 1.

[6] Chuck Swindoll, *Hand Me Another Brick* (Nashville, TN: Thomas Nelson) 1978.

[7] Dr. David Thomas, "Homemade" vol. 15, no. 7, July 1991.

[8] H. Ross Perot, in *Fortune* magazine.

[9] Dean Register, *Minister's Manual*, 1995, p. 339.

[10] Gary Smalley and John Trent, *Husbands and Wives*.

[11] Lois Wyse, *Good Housekeeping*, April 1985.

[12] Dave Barry.

[13] "Have a Good Day" vol. 33, no. 12, April 2001.

[14] *Bits & Pieces*, August 22, 1991.

[15] Gene Solomon.

[16] Ogden Nash.

[17] J. Allen Peterson, "Homemade" vol. 15, no. 5, May 1991. ·

[18] *Bits & Pieces*, October 15, 1992, p. 15-16.

[19] Charles R. Swindoll, *Standing Out*, (Multnomah Press, Portland, OR; 1983), p. 79.

[20] Craig Brian Larson, *750 Engaging Illustrations for Preachers, Teachers, and Writers* (Grand Rapids, MI: Baker Books, 2002), p. 442, quoting from "Bride Gives Groom a Lifesaver in Form of a Transplanted Kidney," *Chicago Tribune*, 10 Nov. 1994, sec. 1, p. 6, "Bride-to-be Promises Hand, Heart — and Kidney to Fiance," *Chicago Tribune*, 10 Oct. 1994, sec. 1, p. 2.

[21] Grady Nutt, *Homemade*, July, 1990.

[22] Charlotte Mortimer, *Reader's Digest*, February 1990.

Simple Living

Photo Credits